TURTLE POINT PRESS
NEW YORK

# TONY SANDERS
# WARNING
# TRACK

I would like to express my deepest gratitude to my
publisher, Jonathan Rabinowitz, for his patience
and care. I would also like to thank Richard
Howard, Langdon Hammer, Robert Zaretsky,
David Lazar, Lynn Doyle and so many others
for their support and encouragement. This book
is dedicated to Matthew, Jack and Linda.

Many thanks to the editors of the publications
in which the following poems have appeared
or are forthcoming: *Cold Mountain Review*:
"Irrecoverable," "Diner"; *Hotel Amerika*: "Cloud
Judgment"; *Paris Review*: "Cordless," "Dirigible,"
"Fish and Blood," "Hard Kind," "Reprises,
Reprisals," "Republic," "Sunday Baroque,"
"The Warning Track"; *Poetry*: "Salt Airs,"
"1998"; *Southwest Review*: "Drunks," "Reeds,"
"Occasional"; *Western Humanities Review*:
"Dusk Song," "War Correspondence,"
"What We Don't"; *Yale Review*: "Holy."
"The Warning Track" also received the
Bernard F. Conners Prize for the long poem.

Design and composition by Jeff Clark
at Wilsted & Taylor Publishing Services

# CONTENTS

## ONE

## TWO

## THREE

## EPILOGUE

# ONE

# LIES

What is vague remains vague,
but the truth goes on insistent, undetected,
without guile, while on the buggy surface
pockets of resistance wait until the trance
is temporarily lifted, until the soon-to-be-forgotten
context appears.

The mind still wants its due, however specific.

What is intimacy but a shell, the walls of a room
to run one's hands down in envy and awe.
Yesterday is today with some improvements,
new furnishings or the rearrangement of old ones
from storage, until the delivery man knocks
with flowers of welcome, albeit with no note.

Candy-coated exhilarations are followed
by an ancient torpor arriving not to be believed
or deciphered. The unstated import is ever-present,
but bashful knowing it too is in the process
of outliving its shelf life.
                              Better to scroll down
the artwork on the inside of a closed eyelid
in silence than to talk about it.

Today is kind, but each moment is unrepentant,
undermining the senses like orange zest
at the cutting board. The mind
unbuttons its determination and gets edgy,
has half-hearted thoughts of winning the lottery
though there is no ticket, no invitation
to shuffle up to the makeshift dais and grab the check.

It takes a while to fold up and pack
the old way of looking at life and move on,
fearful of having nothing more than the memory
of leaving a set of keys dangling in a slightly open door.

The idea that faith has outlived its usefulness
persists, the tin of dependable balm behind the mirror
has hardened. The promise to do better again next time
lacks lustre.

The standing-room-only high drama has been replaced
by dull civility. However late the guests linger, night
makes subtle arrangements for its own exit.

How could one be so far along and yet so tender.

Certain times of day give off an odor,
not the stench of a dead animal, not the reek

of waste or perfume of lilac, not the musk of crotch,
just a telltale whiff to catch our attention before it's gone,
beyond the next bend before we can identify it.

It is our ability to tolerate not knowing
that gets in the way of despair, prompts the pulling up
of a chair to the window to watch what others do,
to make the best of rote.

Are we always indoors, mindful of parkas and mittens,
tinkering with the climate control while waiting
for dinner?

The purpose of any voyage is not the destination,
but the reconnoitering on the couch
years later, with toddlers in the midst
of their own journeys, ever mindful of our own travails
and lies.

# ICONS

The evidence is in arrears.
What has been agreed upon unsightly.
Even an hour of guided meditation totes a penumbra.

Candor has its own logic and vanity,
a habit of searching for a true profile.
It likes what it doesn't see, its plight to be forever out of focus
in a stately office of marble and bone.

The danger of telling the same story
again is telling it the same, so that the lie
has little chance to resurface.

The emotional indices stay calcified, the direction of the day
downturned with the swivel of a desk chair, the tilt
of a screen, the pause of a cursor in the cubicle
long after the boss has gone.

It is enough to be logged on, provided the mind is overseas
stalled in another language, travel being nothing
more than devotion to inertia
in translation.

Now and again the day kicks in, the Mediterranean blue sky
reclaims its borders, its blinking cursor

poised with ambition
and fear.

Only the most faithful tourists do their best to travel
undercover,
to shy away from even modest eye contact,
because clinging to elongated syntax and alternative spellings
buys little time.

There is nothing like dragging icons to the trash.

# THE MURK

Everything slows down,
the threat of groceries, family matters,
each day aswim in its own parabolas, unbeknownst
to the squadron of children on swings
and attendant parents,
the balancing act of youth and decorum.

The answer traipses back, the definitive calm
long awaited arrives somewhat warped,
but not defective.
The hodgepodge is a day-old bouquet, the nuisance
a miracle with parched edges.

There's just enough time to take in
the serenity of jackhammers at a distance, the thought
of an ingot cooling under the tongue fleeting.

Nearby rucksacks and ponchos that fold up at dawn
and reconvene at night are a recurrent theme,
the late-summer squirrels frugal with their opinions
while they trace their own arcs.

Insight changes even as the outlook remains constant
in its murk.

# SUNDAY BAROQUE

The good life is unbuttoned, questions
about gender just stirring after a raucous night
under the hammock. Rumor has it that trellises
and vines have reached an understanding,
even without therapy. Where heroism
and speech-giving will fit in is not quite clear.

For those who are biting their fingernails, why stop there?
Being on the leeward side of today is nothing
more than projection, a heartfelt letter dropped
in the mail without a stamp on purpose.

Tomorrow is predicated on more snoring in the loft,
life as lumpy and comfortable as a flawed quilt.
Each moment has designs on its victims,
but rarely acts. The groan—at hearing the cylinder
catch in the lock of the door—never comes,
the intruder goes back to his dreaming, only to wake again.

There's solace in knowing some days are better than others
for walking with gravel in one shoe, for gazing
at somebody else's impeccably mowed crosshatch of lawn.

Even those of us with the best intentions are preoccupied
by a cowlick, an imaginary rip in the boxers,
anything to keep up the fidgeting
until somebody far too familiar cycles across the grass
with a smile.

# CLOUD JUDGMENT

We all feel it differently but remember it the same,
the explanation of life nothing more than strolling
in a warm coat, her hand in his pocket. The cure
lies sometimes in the thrill of slowing down the pace
though this, we chide ourselves, is mockery of purpose.

The invisible cars glide by in our minds, wagons
that long ago went to shore with tuna on white
stuffed in cellophane, come back as ghosts, as flavors.

To be of two minds is to be transfixed before breakfast,
somewhere between the chilly forecast and roadside fuel spill,
the lozenge dissolving under the tongue, the horse-back
riding way of life an intrigue. Each swashbuckler has his day,
and after the meat of the script, sails home for supper.
What fish would you choose on holiday?

The boulevard turns aghast with itself, the riot on the corner
is a subterfuge, merchants reminding each other of the saga
of time being duplicitous again, as if time would dare
look at itself in the mirror.

And that's just it. The weather is cold and the mittens
making circles on the windowpane are not yours,
though as an aside, there is an invisible, albeit dependable
Aunt Betty busy at the loom. There's always a Betty.

At times the theory of root canals is not a bad thing,
forced entry with a flare, a purpose, another way of expressing
pent-up feelings, a sentimental farewell in the stairwell
as one takes out garbage. There's always garbage.

And if not of two minds, two voices, parallax commandos
in their dotage, talking about the trading of pith
helmets, before the horrifying fact of noon
in the winter heat of indentured dogs and cancelled credit cards.

# OCCASIONAL

In principle he tried to tell the truth,
all the while knowing it did not exist
except for footnotes in books, or credits

too fast to read at the end of the films
people late at night end up sleeping through.
Therein was the rub. He had to admit

nothing, since nothing was the sum total,
the oh-so-eastern side of the equal sign
he had forgotten. But he remembered

plenty. What he wanted was intangible,
evanescent, but often with a twinge
of pain, a theoretical tendon

in an elbow, torn and aggravated
not so much from overuse as neglect,
something to keep him slightly off kilter,

askew, alive. Elements of his life
throbbed inside him and made him uneasy
the way the phantom pain of a lost limb

makes the amputee agonize. Cut off
was what he was, adrift, but the pleasure,
though it was much more comfort or safety,

eluded him. Coming to one's senses,
he thought, was an out-of-reach abstraction.
He liked if that way. Only a masochist,

only a man in the throes of great pain,
would press a finger deep into a bruise
to feel self-inflicted revelations.

In lieu of weather he could choose music
to drift in and out of luminous moods,
or suffer through eerie premonitions

that of late had a way of subsiding
without fanfare. Sometimes a small reward
was the onset of evening and the lamp

left on since dawn drawn to his attention,
sometimes it was the voice of a woman
so far back in the past she must have come

in large part from his imagination.
Sometimes memory has rueful undertows,
as does blood in an aortic valve, or vein,

as does thought in idle contemplation.
Words are wounds, ugly paper cuts, slashes
from boxcutters across the cheek. Meanings

crude sutures a patient pulls out too soon
because of the infected itch for truth.
Often, things do heal of their own accord,

scars form and deform, and oddly stay in place
while one works his way up familial stairs,
and on this of all occasions, just for bed.

# IRRECOVERABLE

All day long he'd been working up the nerve
to tell the truth. By afternoon he thought
better of it. The prospect of being

unfulfilled was fulfilling, the prospect
of at last being fulfilled unnerving.
He was at the center of a story

he reasoned would be of more interest
without him in it. Revision appeared
an easy out as he pictured the glow

of exit signs in the dark, though he knew
he was not leaving. Anyway, travel
of the sort he'd forsaken took planning,

the turning-in of keys to the landlord
and the memory of a place he'd miss.
Not a plush seat but the closed theater,

days sitting alone in the center aisle
waiting for the lure of house lights and brooms.
What if every word were devoid of meaning,

what if every word were nothing more
than an anachronism shouted out
or half-whispered, the stark revelation

that today is just today, the horror
of both insignificance and mass,
thundering applause from an empty house.

Who would have thought time could gloat and cower
at the same time, each of us a sundial
for sale at the back of a flea market,

each of us a radio clock at home,
the blinking of the digital at twelve,
the blinking light forever fixed at noon

until someone takes time to reset it,
to make the minutes match what one can't feel,
the dark hours always in abundance.

# SELF-PORTRAIT

Welcome to the world, he said with a grin,
albeit fiendish. He was lipsync-ing,
in the mirror, of course, with his tuxedo

and high-top sneakers laid out on the bed
behind him. By now, his failures were walking
arm-in-arm in gentle meadows, or else

dozing in deck chairs on the leeward side,
blue ocean equally unperturbed. Why
no one remembered to pack a picnic

blanket remained his mystery. Others
enveloped in undisclosed locations
had the comfort of fingering their fobs

with knowledge that underfoot whole lifetimes
were taking turns turning over new leaves.
What would anybody dare do but smile

back dumbly, as though one had a handle
on the joke? Meanwhile, hordes of decibels
gathering in strategic locations

said hush to each other in expectation
of orders from above. History rewound
and recorded, but what the tape played back

didn't sound quite fair to his tin ears.
Sorrow reverberated for a while
and was replaced by an inkling, again

a sense of something about to go wrong.
Once it was a privilege to be certain of pain,
to be nothing more than alive and feel

the degree and the location, the curse
of healing still in the offing. Often,
it occurred to him to cry out for help

or write a letter of apology
to himself so that he could read it alone
or else, read it aloud in the mirror,

then tear it up, in part thinking someone
down the road might gather up the pieces
and track down the out-of-date zip code.

# IN PROGRESS

Of what was true he was unsure. Thus, he read
himself from memory, and the bright glare
of the first spring afternoon almost became

manageable, the ordinariness
of daily life itself a kind of order
he did not want so much to dwell upon

as to practice leaving off and coming
back to, because it was always brushes
with life that felt right, as though he were

bound to have only an apprenticeship
with his world, the one he could not fathom
along with the one he could, though not with words.

Truth, he found, had a habit of giving way,
clarity became the ultimate inverse
of what was expected, if not hoped for.

# HOLY

The resolve to pray, an inertia
lifted, when all we know is catapulted
across the enemy's bow. For what it's worth,

somebody on the other side of town
may be dropping to his knees, unaware
epiphanies are not in the habit

of sidling up. Shifts in momentum foil
the script, the invisible reader
puts down his bifocals to ponder

the significance of the last passage.
Forgive us, we like what we can't explain
explained, until the truth is carried off

in a bower of nuances. Trumpets blaring
on horseback would be nice. Soldiers
on stretchers salving damp wounds while waiting

for the next ride home would be better. Forged
alliances, the drawing up of fresh
boundaries signals nothing more than new maps

and school satchels, new coordinates
and box lunches for children to mull over
at recess. Each moment in time gets taught

in another, the argument anything
but holy as it travels from the blackboard
to the black eye under the jungle gym.

# SUM

Everything ever known can be reduced
to nothing, all cues removed by standing
still on a broken treadmill someone placed
by the gutter to be picked up. Then what?
Nostalgia for film clips of howitzers?
Cocktail sabers? The future does not wait
on bended knee, but there is a whisper
between today's one-liners and the aspirin.

Somewhere along the way we got too comfy
moving through a series of invisible turnstiles
some of which gave way less readily. The bus
was late, the train lurched out, the cruise ship
stayed anchored offshore. The postage-stamp
way of life we grew up with back home stopped
coming in the mail. Most of us were happy
to avoid the idea of backpedaling on a unicycle.

These current harbors have no boats,
meaning that the rumor has gone inland,
either to lick its wounds in leafy anonymity
or come clean. The impulse is to disengage,
to sit in the back of a baked taverna and watch,
to give in to the aye-aye of second-hand smoke,
waiting for the truth to stand up and identify
itself just once before high-tailing out the door.

# HARD KIND

The prophets on the corner remain aloof,
the marbled beef in their eyes bound for a grill
with no propane. Their wisdom is as closely cropped
as a marine. Not even the hint of pulchritude
atop the cement and mica. Time to kick in
the afterburners and high-tail it to the next idea,
the clearing in the crowd, the sidestreet toward the sun
that sleeps on the river this time of day, of year.
Much of what has happened will be talked about,
cards will be reshuffled, linens changed, a hard kind
of happiness will lurk behind the automated tellers
and subway grates. Only a handful will be entitled
to know their real names, their favorite fruits,
where the best freshets are on the outskirts to dip toes.
It does hurt to speculate, even from the fourth floor,
not knowing what color the next owner will paint
the walls of the brownstone that's boarded up,
or simply not knowing. Adios grandiose. Ta-ta chic.
Could be philosophers are getting used to push brooms.

# TWO

# DIRIGIBLE

Today it's the blimp over Manhattan,
in search of some unnamed event. Drowsy,
gaudy, lazy, almost sexual, its beauty
based on the vulgarity of slow motion
rising above the infinity of other rooftops.

Carefree flight is the opposite of ennui.
Of course, there's more to the lollygagging
than meets the eye: Perish the thought
that the distant dirigible might be adrift,
untethered, askew, off course on purpose.

Not bloated, or besotted, not plump, not
overfed like fowl bred for full-market value,
a solitary figure so far from sleek it's funny
and sad at the same time. An invention
almost mournful over our existence.

# FISH AND BLOOD

Schools of mythical fish twirl in our hearts
because long ago someone stocked the pond.
Maybe there's too much data in the blood.
Not that such angling is rigged. Dice rolls
always favor the house. Yet still we bleed.
We yearn, we pine, we wave our mixed-up rods
like kid conductors in botched rehearsals,
coaxing scales again. Opportunity
knocks, an unexpected tug on the line,
or the western side of the sternum. Heart
drum. Beat of a sad man doing a dance.
Beat of frenzy as fat drips from the spit
to the fire. Hot-blooded, high-pulsed,
it is the fishermen who are cast down.

The halo of gadflies permeated the noontime
which was okay with the harbingers
who had steady work given that golfing
was in season. There were those of us of luck
transcending the box scores of politics
who came down from on high like hang gliders
over the river, but the river said no thank you
so softly and the plush bellies of sails
passed by with some carriage but no children,
and the flavor of the shore was debated.
Cross purposes showed their faces in the clouds
erroneously since the shelf life of sky
changed. Fevers rode taxis free of charge
while in the rear-view mirrors, history blazed.

# DRUNKS

Be seated. How do you begin to sum up such numbers
at this hour of the morning? The Sunday bells
toil both above and beyond, uptown and downtown,
quarreling half-heartedly, or maybe just calling out
to each other, touching base after a murderous week,
even if nobody has died. The inventory of little crimes
adds up and goes unnoticed or hisses with anguish
like the bad spouts of radiators in this room.
If kneeling would help, everybody might ease down
off the folding chairs unlikely to be here next month
or year. The option of gargling with crushed glass
might have been taken up at break were this years ago.
Now that the bells have stopped, listen. Somebody
once raised a hand. Somebody once sighed. All rise.

# DINER

Fenced in by the whale-back of an omelette
whose belly full of cheese might be breathing
slightly, these home fries look dull. Paprika
or even a drizzle of tabasco
shaken out by a shaking hand for spice
won't work, won't perk up the customer's mouth
now chewing on a slice of what the cook
calls *whiskey down.*

　　　　　　　Nevertheless, the grub
form-fits the elongated oval of the plate,
the plate befits the long hour ahead
when time turns into a narrow crawl-space
someone thinking backward might call a tomb,
an overcast day with more hot coffee,
sweet cream and lies floating to the surface.

# RICOCHET

Either the red hammer will strike the nail
square, driving it halfway into the wall,
a wall with the skin of a bomb or burn
victim, so that the bar's artist can claim
space for the maimed face on stretched canvas—
or else just miss, the metal projectile
bouncing back across the glass and thick smoke
into the eye of a stranger, bull's-eye
in the pupil of a drinker in a stupor,
until the lash of pain and shock triggers
an outburst of anger that doesn't stop
but spreads up and down the bar as each fist
fishes for the shot glass or bottleneck,
and a voice cries out, and a bottle pours.

# WHAT WE DON'T

The trance is not over, just easing up.
Even the pools in the suburbs sense it,
now that the tribe is back in the city,
now that the tarps have been hauled from the sheds.
Fat apples are on the lookout again,
grass in the meadow has turned reticent.
It's not easy to be blasé about
miracles, but we try, we put on airs
and turn our backs from some ungodly wind.
Meanwhile, the real simoom gathers inside,
making us just edgy enough for flight.
The automatic skimmers meandering
from side to side in search of silt or scum,
they know by intuition what we don't.

# WAR CORRESPONDENCE

They said *arrondissements* in another country.
Furthermore, in another time, hats had felt brims.
God, a jalopy of sorts, was being fine-tuned
down at the garage, whenever that was.
People were accustomed to corresponding
in painstakingly correct drafts someday
to be found in the hands of archivists with skin
the color of the paper of the letters themselves.
So be it. War was going to break out anyway.
Waiters weren't worried about their tips.
If only everything could have stayed
as orderly and idyllic as those perfect slices
floating on the surface of far-off fingerbowls.
If only mail from abroad had arrived in time.

# PRESCRIPTION

Since today is a pill, we should take it
to feel impervious to life. The right
kind of money can buy new thinking.
If only our internal organs had a tan,
in particular the brain. The relief
is knowing while now's an experiment
forever awaiting federal approval,
no matter what, sleep is in the offing.
Experts are popping them too. The spectre
of opinion is everywhere, waiting
to be phrased like a question, or a smile
mustered by the grim doctor at bedside.
Even when talk is not of living will,
the heart listens closely, with great restraint.

# REPUBLIC

So many channels to choose from. Somewhere
in the high numbers, blockheads trash-talk
during recess in the blue playground near school.
Thumb down the dial by remote and find
their doppleganger echoes via dish, the same
kids in the same setting. Along the way, the present
and past bound together like kitsch and Christ.
Wasn't there once something beautiful about
the black-&-white eye of the test pattern open
late at night until the predicated hour of morning
when the sudden countdown from ten to one
in the screen-encompassing orb on the Zenith
or Philco meant nothing more than a kid's comfort
before the airing of the anthem, the liftoff of day.

# REEDS

History defeats itself again and again, and here we crouch,
outpatients in the duck blinds peeling back the reeds,
trying to get a glimpse of kindred spirits taking flight,
aware that only yesterday our senses were shotgunned.
For so long it seemed we were under the observation
of an invisible expert with stellar credentials who gave out
day passes. Perhaps the animal in us just petered out,
or waded down the coast for calmer waters. Tourists
gathered like hunters on the bluff, but the threat of rain
or bell for grub drove them off. Where do we go from here?
The causeway back to the mainland? The sunken dinghy?
Maybe the consolation of stars will come later on the beach
after we build a fire, not so much to warm our palms
as to signal to anyone in sight we're no longer decoys.

# CORDLESS

O to be telephoned late at night by a stranger whose voice
projects nothing but bright concern, nothing intimate
between you except a common regard for the hour
that passes like a game of solitaire in a dark kitchen.
Who wouldn't want the attention? The gas-blue torpor
of the range abandoned for the invisible quasar of comfort
coming from someone just as iffy on the downtown side
of your universe. The transmission of knowledge or love
might pale in contrast to a bridge built largely on talk
and silence. Cordless, you might make your way to bed
with the receiver at your ear so that when there is nothing
further to be said, no more need to console one another,
you can say goodbye knowing there is good reason
for conversation that begins in mystery and ends with sleep.

# SEASIDE

It's the toothpick we've been working lately,
it's the plastic cup of butter and the dirty bib
after the cracking of claws, after the meat.
Not that the conversation over victuals
midday down at surf side doesn't matter.
Anyone can voice opinions about neap tides
or the empty abodes of shellfish. The sagas
people grow fond of are bound to roll up
their invisible khakis and drift out of sight.
Uncomplicated, yes, until one recalls the sun,
dependable old diastole in a noon mood
until it opts for the other side of a sea wall
or dune. Uncomplicated, no, given an ocean
often troubled by its own hunger and retreat.

# SALT AIRS

Time not being an issue, he'd probably write.
You know the type of letters people send from the coast.
First, it might be the invisible room service he'd summon
to raise the dormer. Since salt air does for thoughts
what salt does to a wound, he would ask for his chair,
a wicker one as white as a cumulonimbus cloud,
to face the open window. From the bed,
a four-poster at the far wall with a white spread,
he could stretch out and study the still life
of an empty chair in an open-ocean afternoon until
someone from memory unexpectedly knocked on the door
to slip a white envelope more than halfway underneath
only to reconsider and pull it back. Maybe he'd frown
at the tide of unfinished correspondence. Maybe he'd write.

# DUSK SONG

Nothing that I did, or said,
made me approachable. People glared,
perhaps because of my desire to put things in order.
It was the way I was taught thus I taught
others as if I were crazy, held sway.
Maybe I should have scuttled home.

Called to myself in the third person
as if He were once my ally.
My short-lived rapture,
such fragile distancing from myself all for nought.
Now I know how both of them—of us!—
licked the dasher of vanilla cream, and licked pus.

Bones? What about my coat of bones
wrapped up cold at the end of the bench.
Once it was just a boy on a swing
in a pair of short pants, and I swung,
in an ever-increasing arc.
O even the best parks grow dark.

# SHOPPING

"You pays, you owns, no changes here, no cash
back neither, no tit for tat, and no touching
the merchandise, get that?"
Customers are squeezing. Everyone's
hassled. The barker atop the sidewalk ladder:
ever seen someone madder?

Imagine a dime in the palm of a kid, his vice grip
taught, as he sidles down aisles of fabric,
linen and polyester,
bins of scarves entwined like snakes, bins
of body parts in the back, a scene from Bosch,
them mannequins.

Big sale or big deal? Big man. Big lie.
All is legal and all is good. Or did the man
say goods? Time's up, kid.
Bite the bullet, or in this case, coin.
You'd better catch up to mommy's cotton,
or be forgotten.

# REPRISES, REPRISALS

The game is tone, ironic peal, some would say
moans, or cheap banter, a few promises
to recurrent nemeses,
to troglodytes and muses. Heady stuff,
pilgrim. What's the antidote for shame,
honesty in the wake of fame?

White lie at a time when the truth might slip,
a little sin to keep the lowdown down,
half-truth, waffle,
innuendo out of the mouth of a liar. Script
tease, perhaps. The body of work a burlesque
against meaning.

The take-off is a put-on at the start,
the only catch the fear of getting caught
coming clean, that's all.
Reprises, reprisals.
Rogue royale, the foul owl who growls and scowls,
he weeps in the dark.

# LOCAL HISTORY

You said the house had wings, but you meant more,
not that there were bats upside down above you,
although that's what the neighbors chose to think

when they looked out from black windows like owls.
That was some years ago. Many parlances ago.
You get the feeling if you could ride the bus back

to what has long been torn down and trucked away
there might be clues like relics for the archeologist
to take back to the lab, something very personal.

Landscapes don't die, but the look of them does,
the flag still waving just as always in a familiar yard
seems out of place, as if suddenly it has no right

to be there, although in reality it could be just you
projecting your own dizzying sense of displacement
on an inanimate object, on an ordinary flagpole.

Just like that the emotion goes, and you wonder
whether it's worth piecing everything back together.
In a way, you have no choice but to move forward,

but there's always that desire to be astonished
like a toddler in a stroller pointing and shouting
*house*, pointing at the sky and shouting *wings*.

# NO MERLOT

Everything's out of whack. Tenants walk down
the street for dinner, but what's in it for kids
except the jungle straw with a large shake.
Logic paces to and fro in the eyes
of cats in windows with venetians closed.
Soon it will be time for dessert and forgetting,
the evening vast and unpopulated.
Time to be thankful and water the plants,
pinch the wilted buds. Things could get much worse,
the doctrine of shorter days takes precedence
over a tête-à-tête between lovers
living in separate apartments. Mail might
start piling up in front of neighbors' doors.
It's never too late to start preparing
the next robust meal, the threat of a guest
welling up long before the hunger. Time
to dust off the landlord's best wine. Put it back.

# BANQUET

Knowing what others must be thinking smarts,
puts a damper on the meal, puts a cork
in the bottle, so that even before the *tarte*,
even before the coffee, side exits
seem right. There are other ways to review
the banquet, to put into perspective
the hand that in memory slides up the thigh
after the first course and finger bowl,
then vanishes, the impulse second-guessed
or perhaps frightened away. The menu
doesn't change, the guest list gets fine-tuned
from time to time in the off hours, names
bandied about until wet tea leaves pick
a keynote speaker with nothing to say
until he steps to the lectern and sighs,
exile from a country that never was.

# COASTAL

My passport would like to meet your passport,
maybe exchange numbers, set up a date
for lunch on the quai. By the time the sun
turns into butter on the horizon,
we'll be bilingual. Funny how most fez
moments crop up on the coast. Here it is
the off-season with only beachcombers,
a community of nudes from someplace
like Alsace or Erie holing up in caves
to the south. Protocol calls for champagne
or a plastic glass of anise and water
to be raised in honor of foreigners
as evanescent as clouds in translation.
Souls have a penchant for gliding in reverse.

# OFFAL

Someone is bivouacking as we speak,
lugging left-handed machetes upland in darkness,
nostalgic for the finery of shawls and awnings
while hacking down fronds.
Someone is staring dumbfounded
at the beeper dropped in the deep end of the pool.
Impervious to truth,
we keep dreaming of new ways to get derailed,
since we believe detours are not the close relatives
of dead ends.
After the invisible parfait
comes a skinful of veggie haggis plopped on the plate,
followed by prayers,
desperate tonguing in the garden.
Before the orchestra gets catapulted back to old habits,
the aftertaste of any era seems brackish,
anything but pleasant, or sane.

# THREE

# THE WARNING TRACK

I

Baseball is the purest sport, meaning
ballparks out in the heartland, mixing
forkballs and slurves, tapping
slow choppers in a spring rain.
Winter locked us out, covering
the infield in aphasic snow, leaving
the bases sticking out like square tubers.
Summer surprised us, coming over the left field fence
like a shower of beer; we stopped in the entry tunnel,
and walked out in sunlight, into the bleachers,
and drank slowly, and studied the lineups.
'Batting third and playing right field, Ike Deutsch.'
And when we were children, over at the neighbors',
my friend swung and accidentally hit me in the head.
And he was frightened. He said, Mary,
are you all right? And down I went
as if my head were a mountain, my body the sea.
I bled much of the night, and went home in the morning.

What are the hits that matter, what logic of numbers
rises from this dusty diamond? Listen, man,
you cannot say for sure whether it's ball or strike
when the catcher's in the way, and the bat swings,
and the full house is yelling, the temperature over 100,

and the corners of home plate obscured. Only
there is intelligence behind this steel mask,
(look into the eyes behind this steel mask),
and you can see something different from either
the pitcher's face leaning forward to read the signs
or the seams of the ball as it breaks away from you.
Step out of the box and pick up a handful of dust.

> *Where have you gone*
> *Joe DiMaggio?*
> *Our nation turns*
> *Its lonely eyes to you.*

'You took me to the stadium first a year ago;
you said I was going to be an all-star.
—Yet when we came back, late, from behind the bleachers,
your hands dirty and your pants wet, I would not
talk, my skirt torn, I was neither
home nor away, and I saw nothing,
looking into the middle of the dash, but darkness.'

Old Abdullah, famous oddsmaker,
didn't exist, nevertheless
is regarded as the best in the business
of wicked picks on points. Here, he said,
is your card, a 1951 Ralph Branca
(Willie Mays was on deck. Remember!).
Here is the kissing bandit from Baltimore,

the lady of force plays at second.
Here is the man with three fingers, Mordecai Brown,
and here is the midget, and this card,
which is blank, can win you something if you scratch
off the surface. If you don't find
The Commissioner, you don't win.
I see bettors milling around the window.
Careful. If you see the one we call Brooklyn,
tell him I'll bring the results myself:
Tell him to be careful.


Shea Stadium,
under the light smog of a winter dawn,
a subway lumbered into the elevated station, a few
figures got off and started walking, though not many.
Eyes above turned-up collars, hands in pockets,
each of them keeping distance from the next.
Pushed through the turnstiles and past the token booth
where a woman with fingerless gloves looked down
with the clock behind her unreadable under grafitti.
Saw someone I recognized from my neighborhood
and stopped him, saying, 'Rudy, we did games together,
do you still buy cheap seats and move up to the boxes
or do you now pay? Want to go again next season?
Or do you no longer think of baseball in the bed of winter?
We could go back to where we dug under the fence,
although now it's impenetrable with poured concrete!'
I am one of you! You are one of us! You are guilty too!

## II

The chair he leaned forward in was of well worn leather,
especially the arm rests where his elbows went,
when they weren't stretched out before him on the formica,
or beckoning the cameraman in black headphones
to come out from behind a camera to answer a question,
the stadium lights reduced into one bright block
tripled in the blue-black glass of the zoom's outer lens
and the distorted silhouette of his own image included
as he was turned away from the microphone.
From the stands a synesthesia of sound and movement,
the panoply of color in distant stands an imitation
of Seurat one minute, and Pollock the next.
An enormous television screen in center field, a film clip
of a legend sliding slow-motion into second base,
shown three times, each increasingly larger,
until the frame froze on a foot, a base and a mitt.
Which dissolved into a close-up of a woman
walking awkwardly in high heels across the infield
to a microphone placed on the rubber of the mound,
the players nearby at attention, indifferent, at each bag.
Which dissolved into a close-up of a flag out in center
artificially fluttering in the still night air, as if at gunpoint.
And the singer sang the song with an inviolable voice,
and some fans sang, some just mouthed the words
'O say does that . . . wave' to dirty ears.
And so many gestures from the garden of evening
appearing randomly from billboard to billboard,

under the ballpark lights, in the midst of noise,
the applause peppered with signs and slogans,
as the broadcaster looked out, and held his breath,
before he announced the orders, while looking ill.

'The stands are filled tonight. Yes, filled. Stay tuned.
The ballclub is out of the cellar. Stay tuned. Stay.
It's a beautiful night for baseball, don't you think?
I feel like they're going to change their luck, don't you?'

Anybody still left in his or her right mind
knows we're all going down the chute, n'est-ce pas?

'What's that?'
                    The airplanes circling LaGuardia.
'That too, coming from the north?'
                                        Traffic over traffic.

'It's not like it was. It wasn't like this. Do you
remember—'
                    'Nothing.'
I remember
checkers to the ballpark, the over and under.
'You remember Abdullah; there's nothing he wouldn't—'
                                                        'Debt.'

Meanwhile the television over the bar,
and the radio speakers flanking the door.
'Maybe we should bag it. Like yesterday.

'Give tomorrow a fair chance.'
                                        Aspirin at ten.
And if the game is rained out,
we'll have no reason for going out,
looking out the window and waiting alone for the evening news.


When Charlie got laid off the first of the month, I said—
I s'pose I'd had a few, I said to him in his ear,
THE CONSUMER INDEX ROSE TWO TENTHS OF ONE PERCENT
we have a little to fall back on, plus what I've saved.
But I didn't want to go into that right off, didn't want him
knowing
                what I had
as if I'd been stealing. Or hiding it from the sharks.
I couldn't stand watching him settle into the couch,
day after day so depressed, I thought, with the TV going,
'One Life to Live. Jenny Jones. As the World Turns. Oprah.
The Guiding Light. Geraldo. Sally Jesse Raphael. Donahue.'
Tired of this routine with donuts and beer, I said,
get a life, you ought to be ashamed, you act like you're retired.
(And him only thirty-one.)
If you don't like it, he says in that voice of his, you can stuff it.
FIVE-DAY FORECAST CALLS FOR UNSEASONABLY MILD
TEMPERATURES
And then, I can't help, hun. With that sad face I married.
I keep thinking there's a chance he'll get off the couch.
In the beginning I could perk him up with take-out.
(It's been weeks now. Maybe he should get on The Couch.)
Ever since he got laid off it hasn't been the same.

You are the enabler, I said to myself.
If you can't get him out of the house you've got to start thinking
of your own preservation.
You didn't get married to take care of an invalid, did you?
LOCAL NINES MAKE DEAL
MORE DETAILS AT ELEVEN
It's after six thirty. Got to be going. Say hi to Phil for me.
Same to Bob. Call me if you need anything. I mean it, really.
Okay? Okay, thanks. See ya. Yea. Later.


# | | |


The avenue is quiet: the deepening whir of a taxi
slightly comforting as it glides to a halt. Here and there,
steam dances out of a manhole and disperses. The drunks are
   in doorways,
curled up and crooked like tamped-out cigarettes.
Even the wide O's in 'Houston' and 'Bowery' suggest someone
in no hurry to have the sweet fire in his stomach burn out after
   a swig,
someone with eyes not of pearl, but of vitreous oyster
embedded in lidskin as black and lax as the labia of a stray.
The bell-rope that wakes up the city each day is busted,
the church's parapets obscured under workmen's netting.
Have empathy for the recalcitrance of the winter sun
on the other side of the eyebrows of old law tenements.
Have empathy for the old bones still willing to be warmed.

Gulls poked discriminatingly through the landfill
touching down and taking off again and again as if it were too hot
as I drove one weeknight recently through the outskirts
going nowhere in particular with the radio off and window down
thinking about playing catch with my brother years ago
when we could still play pretend games for hours
on an abandoned diamond next to a scrap metal dealer
with rust-colored rivulets running under the corrugated partition
    into the infield.
The wince and shriek of twisting iron was deafening.
Once we looked inside and saw the purgatorial foreman
in a rubber coat and boots wading through a slush of water and ore
and behind him a crane with a magnetic disk picking up a wreck.

I am one of you
you are one of us
you are guilty too
tra la la la la

Shea Stadium
under the light smog of a winter dusk
by the ticket booths near the north entrance
Monsieur Claude the merchant man
Senor Sir Cloud sold me two grams of coke
sight unseen, C.O.D., only stepped on twice
he said, walking me toward the downtown local.

The only ignominy is old age,
the body as withering and insignificant

as a camphor ball in the back corner of a closet,
unless you do something about it.
Even if you do something about it.
There. That's better. And already it's behind you
with the velocity of a sentence you just said.
I get the distinct feeling we're all condemned
to lean our elbows on the second-floor window sill
waiting for the world's kettle of water to boil.
O sure, there are the usual diversions,
the balms, salves and recipes handed down
slightly different from generation to generation
like the recuperation narratives they come with.
But that's just it. History shows up with a facelift
and shades, and nobody here can identify him.
Children tell time by schoolbus or the minute hand
of a mother walking them briskly off to kindergarten.

HURRY UP CHILD
HURRY UP CHILD WE'RE LATE
They are too young to be indifferent enough to life.
Think of how the heads of commuters all bob alike
according to curves and dips in the road they know by rote.
Meanwhile, the romance of the skyline flies by unnoticed,
except when Him tells Her 'that's the house that Ruth built'
trying to start a conversation before she gets off in Pelham....

The part of the day seeming christened,
and maybe chastened. The promise of
morning, the uptempo of sunrise streaking

the shady bedroom is removed, is remote.
Why? Why does the sheet and pillow bower
of dawn always get stunned awake, then
tossed aside? What happens to the liquid
fear commuting from sleep to the surface?

The kiosk and straphandle and ledge of curb.
The abacus of oranges flowing out of a mart.
The cortical torture of a triggered auto alarm.
O City city, the fish knives of Fulton Street
de-bone and fillet on the other side of the river,
though the South Street cinema runs a replica
two blocks from the vangs of a stalled tall ship;
no sign of hasty caulking, no barnacles, no mold.

The music in the alley
and the music in the street
and the music in the subway
ain't the music in the heat.

   *Of course every boy has a sweetheart,*
    *And some boys they have two or three.*

White men, black men,
Koreans, spics and chinks
none of us can get along
so everybody stinks.

   *Of all the girls in this great city,*
    *There is only one in it with me.*

Boom box, ball cap,
executive-style tie,
people in the city
never look you in the eye.

>   *She lives with her folks on The Bowery*
>   *A few doors away from Canal,*

Tristan and Wystan
where did you go?
You should have stuck around
til the end of the show.

>   *And helps to support her mother*
>   *Does my little Bowery gal.*

Yes, Walt,
what it is then between us
but always the sea and the railing railing railing.

The railing.


# IV

X had been holed up in his study much too long
trying to put the finishing touches on his masterpiece.
Sooner or later he had to look up from his invisible escritoire
and summon the chaffeur for a drive in the country,

and maybe a stroll in the state park to cure his insouciance.
It's not that he put the desk in front of the wrong window,
(he had already experimented in all four directions)
rather that the unfinished oeuvre had made him a ghost writer,
despite the fact that he was the subject of his own work.
The excursion out of the city made him feel as anonymous
and insignificant as a footnote in the back of a lost tome.
There was something nostalgic about light weekend traffic,
the monochromatic veil of dreary buildings by the highway.
It was as if it had been this way a long time and the landscape
of smokestacks and warehouses and parched ball fields
was hibernating or suffering from chronic fatigue syndrome.
Such spontaneous junkets did not go too far from home,
the apogee of these empty epics only an hour or two away.
The idea of going out and coming back from no destination
with someone else at the wheel was an alternative to breathing.


V


Data?
What about the data
we lost when we didn't press 'Save'
and a surge from the thunder brought down the system.
Could we regroup
and reconstruct the narrative as it was
complete with those spontaneous digressions we found
sitting together in the stands of an abandoned ballpark
one weekday in the middle of winter
and later leaning against the chain-link fence by the dugout

looking at what was left of the almost eroded pitcher's mound
the rubber awkwardly exposed like a gum's last tooth
and later walking in the outfield with a history equally eroded
of teenagers backpedaling on the warning track
oblivious to the slant rhyme of subway cars
and later standing on the place where the plate used to be
and picking up a handful of dust.

Few places are as elegiac as ball fields in winter,
excepting perhaps old amusement parks by the sea in winter,
especially in a rain so light it does not fall as much as materialize.
Isn't this how it is with inspiration,
a slight coating just enough to throw off your perception of the
    familiar
and soon the whole landscape seems formal.

Time is a terminally ill close relative of yours
and your impulse is to take a very good look at every feature
before you go
because tomorrow the bed may be empty.
And so, what is it? What are we meant to infer
from the almost imperceptively slow decline from stable to
serious to critical?
What was the doctor saying when we were in the hall?
Is sadness something we were supposed to get used to?

The beauty of the ball and mitt was that there was no clock,
everything being equal the game could have gone on forever.

# EPILOGUE

# GONDOLA

No more cross-talking in the gondola,
all the glazed eyes focused on the moment
sanity makes a token appearance,
when riders glide under the privileged bridge,
just before the canal makes a dogleg
left. Those of us getting out for lunch
run the risk of getting back in. Nature
has its own good-natured twin
forever tethered in an old quarter
closed to the public. Meanwhile, the water
pooling in a nearby basement ripples
like a shaky chalice filled at midnight
and refilled. Don't we all want slow boat rides?
You can bet the house the easiest route
to open water is common knowledge.
The margin for error is a secret.